The Seaside

Sarah Ridley

W
FRANKLIN WATTS
LONDON • SYDNEY

First published in 2007
by Franklin Watts

Franklin Watts
338 Euston Road
London NW1 3BH

Franklin Watts Australia
Level 17/207 Kent Street
Sydney, NSW 2000

Series editor: Sarah Peutrill
Art director: Jonathan Hair
Design: Jane Hawkins

A CIP catalogue record for this book is available from the British Library.

Dewey number: 790.1
ISBN: 978 0 7496 7066 5

Printed in China

Franklin Watts is a division of Hachette Children's Books.

Picture credits:
Blackpool Central Library: 14, 21.
Colchester Museum Service; 6, 9c,15, 16t, 20.
Mary Evans Picture Library: 8, 9t, 11, 13, 18t, 18b, 24t, 27.
The Francis Frith Collection: 10, 12, 22, 23b, 24b, 25.
NMPFT/Science & Society Picture Library: 26.

Many thanks to the following people for allowing their photos to be used in the book: Lionel Baker 23t; Lucy Bosomworth 19r; Jane Orbell 23t; Jessie Ridley 23t; Nick Ridley 16bl, 19l; Jane Sheena 17 (and cover), 19r; Susie Wigglesworth 23t. Every attempt has been made to clear copyright. Should there be any inadvertent omission please apply to the publisher for rectification.

'Oh I do like to be beside the seaside,
I do like to be beside the sea,
I do like to stroll along the prom, prom, prom,
Where the brass bands plays,
Tiddly-om-pom-pom...'

Victorian music hall song, 1907,
by John A Glover-Kind

Contents

By the sea

At the seaside we build sandcastles, paddle or swim in the sea. Sometimes we go on the pier or eat ice cream. Many things we enjoy at the seaside began in Victorian times, over 100 years ago.

Date: c. 1900

So much is happening in this busy photograph of Clacton-on-Sea. Look for children playing in the sand and paddling, people taking a swim, arriving back from a boat trip, visiting stalls, walking along the promenade and sheltering from the sun.

Seaside timeline

1750 Doctors decide that breathing sea air, swimming in the sea and even drinking seawater are very good for people. Wealthy people visit the seaside for health cures.

c.1750 The bathing machine is invented (see page 14).

1840s onwards Railway stations open in many seaside places. Small seaside villages grow into busy seaside resorts (another name for a seaside town). Wealthy people go for seaside holidays while less wealthy people visit for the day.

1860s onwards Many seaside resorts build piers.

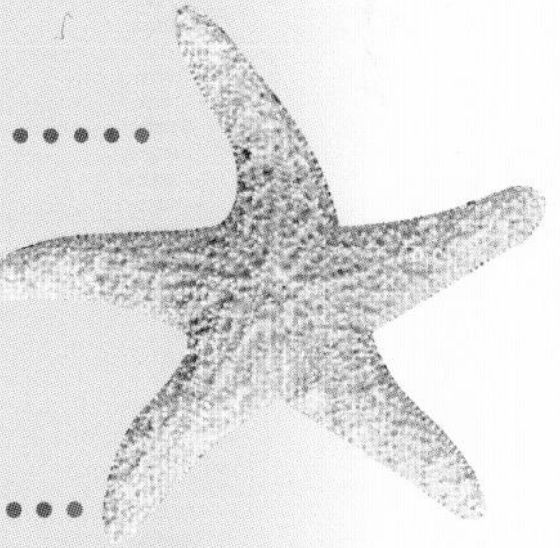

1910 onwards Pier owners build bandstands, theatres and cafés. Then some add cinemas and fairground rides.

1930s More people can afford to go on holiday. Holiday camps open near to the sea.

1939–45 (The Second World War) Some seaside resorts are closed in case of invasion.

1960s and 1970s Many more people go on holiday abroad to countries such as France, Spain, Italy and Greece. In Britain, some piers fall down while others add more rides and amusement arcades.

Today Seaside holidays and day trips remain popular in Britain.

Getting there

In the early 1900s, most people began their journey to the sea at a railway station. By the 1920s, holiday-makers also travelled by charabanc (open-topped bus) or by car. In the 1960s and 1970s, people started to fly to seaside resorts in countries such as Greece and Spain.

Date: 1908

A crowded train brings hundreds of well-dressed passengers to the seaside.

Date: 1912

A steamboat full of London holiday-makers heads for the coast. People who lived in cities such as Glasgow and London could travel by steamboat to the seaside.

Two charabancs set off for a day by the sea. Many churches, schools and work places organised charabanc trips to the seaside.

Date: 1918

Be a history detective

- Are the passengers from the train carrying any luggage? Do you think they are visiting for the day, or staying for the week?
- Why do you think buses took over from charabancs? Think about the weather.

Bed and board

About 100 years ago, many wealthy families stayed in seaside hotels for their holidays. Some less wealthy families saved up all year to afford a few days at the sea. It was cheaper to rent a room in a boarding house than to stay in a hotel.

Date: 1890

Huge hotels, like this one in Brighton, filled up with hundreds of holiday-makers during the summer.

A couple stand outside a boarding house. There were strict rules at many boarding houses about when meals were served and about keeping sand out of the rooms.

Date: 1920s

Be a history detective

- Ask your grandparents whether they ever stayed in a boarding house or a hotel by the sea.
- Compare the hotel and the boarding house. Which would you prefer to stay in?

Chalets and camping

By the 1930s and 1940s, more families could afford to take a holiday at the seaside. Many people preferred the new holiday camps to hotels and boarding houses. In the 1960s, camping and caravanning became popular.

Sports' day at a holiday camp in Scarborough. People stayed in the chalets that surround the green. There were lots of things to do at the camps, which had boating lakes, entertainers and huge swimming pools.

Date: c. 1955

Tents and caravans at a campsite right by the sea.

Date: 1960s

Be a history detective

- Did your parents go to a holiday camp or campsite when they were young? What can they remember?
- How can you tell that the camping photograph was taken a long time ago? Start by looking at the cars.

Sea swimming

The Victorians did not like to show off their bodies, so people changed inside bathing machines. Slowly people stopped using bathing machines and many more people swam in the sea.

The huts on wheels are Victorian bathing machines. Look for the horses that pulled the machines into the sea so people could swim in private.

Date: 1890

A raft in the sea provides lots of fun for these swimmers. Some seaside resorts also built open-air swimming pools by the sea.

Be a history detective

- Compare how many people are swimming in each of these photographs.
- What things do people play with in the sea today? Are they like the sea raft?

Swimwear

A hundred years ago people kept themselves covered at the beach. Most people only wore swimsuits to go swimming. Gradually people wore fewer clothes and swimwear became more comfortable.

Date: 1912

Two children wear swimsuits almost down to their knees. The rest remain fully dressed.

Date: 1942

A boy wears a swimsuit made of wool. Boys, as well as girls, wore swimsuits with straps in the 1930s and 1940s.

Twins keep cool wearing bikinis made of nylon.

Be a history detective

- Look closely at the oldest photograph to see what children wore at the beach.
- Wool gets heavy when it is wet. How do you think it felt to wear a swimsuit like the one in the 1942 photograph?

On the sand

In the past children enjoyed building sandcastles, as they do today. Some children paddled, swam or searched for shells. Others played games while their parents and grandparents relaxed.

Date: 1905

A hundred years ago, many boys sailed toy wooden boats at the seaside.

Children build sandcastles on the beach. Their spades are made from wood and metal.

Date: 1913

Date: 1942

A boy searches for shells to put in his metal bucket.

Date: 1974

A girl enjoys the sand boat that her sister is building.

Be a history detective

- In the past, buckets and spades were made from wood and metal. What are your bucket and spade made of?
- Which of these things do people like to do at the seaside today?

The promenade

The Victorians loved to stroll along the promenade after spending time on the beach. Some people walked along the promenade to a fairground, such as the Blackpool Pleasure Beach. Others visited parks, cafés, shops or the pier.

Date: 1900

Lots of people sit and enjoy the view of the sea, or watch others stroll along the promenade.

Date: 1914

There was so much to do at Blackpool Pleasure Beach, including taking rides on the helterskelter (right) and the big wheel (centre).

Be a history detective

- Look for prams in the 1900 picture. Are they like pushchairs and prams today? How are people dressed for walking on the promenade?
- What would you choose to do at the Pleasure Beach? Look for the rollercoaster. It is in the distance with a flag on top.

Piers

Piers were built at many seaside resorts in Victorian times. Gradually, pier owners built dance halls, bandstands, theatres and even fairground rides to entertain people. In the 1960s, many piers fell down because they were old. Most were not rebuilt.

People stroll along the pier at Clacton-on-Sea. Steamboats from London unloaded passengers at the end of the pier.

Be a history detective

- Ask some adults about visiting the pier. Did they go on rainy or sunny days?
- Read the signs on the 1907 pier to see what people could do there.
- How has Clacton pier changed between 1907 and 1960 (see right)?

Date: 1950

A family snapshot of a visit to Clacton pier. Steel Stella, a rollercoaster, is behind them.

This is Clacton-on-Sea on a sunny day, ten years later. You can see the pier with buildings for penny-slot machines, an aquarium, cafés, the rollercoaster and other rides.

Date: 1960

Beach entertainment

In the early 1900s, entertainers performed on the beach. People told jokes, sang songs or danced. There were puppet shows and donkey rides. Some of these entertainments are still around today.

Date: 1905

Children prepare for a donkey ride along the beach.

Date: 1912

White-faced pierrots perform on a special stage above the beach.

Adults and children enjoy a Punch and Judy puppet show.

Be a history detective

- Look at how people are dressed in the photographs. It is a good way of working out how long ago a photograph was taken.
- You can still enjoy Punch and Judy shows and donkey rides in some seaside resorts. Have you seen them? Why do you think these entertainments have lasted?

Picnics and treats

Many people have always taken a picnic with them for a day out to the seaside. Your grandparents may remember stalls selling seafood, such as cockles and oysters, or buying fish and chips wrapped in newspaper. They probably bought ice cream between wafers.

Date: 1899

A family picnic around a boat on the beach.

Children enjoy ice creams on the beach. They are eating them with flat wooden spoons.

Date: 1955

Be a history detective

- Look at the oldest photograph. How is one woman staying out of the sun?
- Talk to your parents and grandparents about what they ate at the seaside.

Souvenirs

A souvenir can be a postcard, a toy, a food item, a special shell or almost anything that reminds you of where you have been. What souvenirs have you brought back from holidays or days out?

People often send postcards from holidays or days out. Can you put these in order, from oldest to newest?

Answer: A, C, B

Glossary

Amusement arcade A room or hall where you can play on penny-slot, pinball and other machines.

Aquarium A building where you can see living fish, plants and other water creatures in large tanks.

Bandstand A raised platform, with a roof, where concerts are performed.

Big wheel A fairground ride. People pay to sit in seats attached to a giant wheel that moves round and round.

Boarding house A large house where visitors can rent rooms for a few nights or weeks from a landlord or landlady.

c. (circa) This means 'about' and is used with a date, for example c.1920, when it isn't known exactly when something happened.

Charabanc An open-topped bus, popular in the 1920s and 1930s.

Cockles Shellfish that you can eat.

Dance hall A place where people paid a small amount of money to go to dance.

Helterskelter A fairground ride. People pay to ride on a small mat down a huge spiral slide.

Oysters Shellfish that you can eat.

Pierrot Entertainers who covered their faces in white make-up, dressed as clowns and performed singing and dancing shows.

Promenade A long path for walking beside the sea.

Punch and Judy A puppet show about Mr Punch and his wife, Judy.

Resort A town or village beside the sea that people like to visit for a day trip or a holiday.

Steamboat A passenger boat powered by steam engines.

Index

Further information

Books

Ways Into History: Seaside Holidays by Sally Hewitt (Franklin Watts)

Start-Up History: Seaside Holidays by Stewart Ross (Evans)

Websites

http://home.freeuk.com/elloughton13/seaside.htm
Snaith Primary School website which allows you to visit eight different seaside resorts and take a picture tour of Blackpool.

http://www.francisfrith.com/gallery/7
Use this photo library to look at photos of seaside places in the past.

http://tife.org.uk/clicker/flashhistoryks1/seaside.swf
The website of the Lighthouse for Education has lots of information about seaside holidays in the past.

Note to parents and teachers: Every effort has been made by the Publishers to ensure that these websites are suitable for children, that they are of the highest educational value, and that they contain no inappropriate or offensive material. However, because of the nature of the Internet, it is impossible to guarantee that the contents of these sites will not be altered. We strongly advise that Internet access is supervised by a responsible adult.